The Friage Is Being Rude

Level 8 – Purple

Helpful Hints for Reading at Home

The graphemes (written letters) and phonemes (units of sound) used throughout this series are aligned with Letters and Sounds. This offers a consistent approach to learning whether reading at home or in the classroom. Books levelled as 'a' are an introduction to this band. Readers can advance to 'b' where graphemes are consolidated and further graphemes are introduced.

HERE IS A LIST OF ALTERNATIVE GRAPHEMES FOR THIS PHASE OF LEARNING. AN EXAMPLE OF THE PRONUNCIATION CAN BE FOUND IN BRACKETS.

Phase 5 Alternative Pronunciations of Graphemes			
a (hat, what)	e (bed, she)	i (fin, find)	o (hot, so)
u (but, unit)	c (cat, cent)	g (got, giant)	ow (cow, blow)
ie (tied, field)	ea (eat, bread)	er (farmer, herb)	ch (chin, school, chef)
y (yes, by, very)	ou (out, shoulder, could, you)		
o_e (home)	u_e (rule)		

HERE ARE SOME WORDS WHICH YOUR CHILD MAY FIND TRICKY.

Phase 5 Tricky Words			
oh	their	people	Mr
Mrs	looked	called	asked
could			

TOP TIPS FOR HELPING YOUR CHILD TO READ:

- Allow children time to break down unfamiliar words into units of sound and then encourage children to string these sounds together to create the word.
- Encourage your child to point out any focus phonics when they are used.
- Read through the book more than once to grow confidence.
- Ask simple questions about the text to assess understanding.
- Encourage children to use illustrations as prompts.

This book is a 'b' level and is a purple level 8 book band.

The Fridge Is Being Rude

Written by
John Wood

Illustrated by
Chloe Jago

Papa Wang was sitting in his chair. It was a lovely day in June and the house was quiet. It was time for a nice cup of tea.

Suddenly his niece, Yan, burst into the room. She was trying not to giggle. "Papa! The fridge is talking and it's saying rude words!" said Yan.

They both went to the kitchen. Papa Wang opened the fridge door.
"Smelly snot drips!" said the fridge.
"Excuse me?" said Papa Wang. He was shocked. Then, the fridge said…

Papa Wang quickly closed the door. "How rude," he said. "I've no clue why this is happening. Do not tell anyone about this, Yan. I'm sure it will stop soon."

The next day, there was a knock on the door. The whole town was outside. There was a queue all the way down the street!
"We hear your fridge is being rude," said Sue, who lived next door.

"I didn't tell anyone, I swear!" said Yan.
"I do not think that is true," said Papa Wang.
"Bottom breath!" said the fridge.

Someone knocked on the door. It was a small man. "Hello, my name is Luke. I hear your fridge is being rude. Can we put it in a film?" said Luke.

"There must be someone who can fix it," said Papa Wang as he looked on the computer.
"Nobody can fix this," giggled Yan.
"You soggy cake!" said the fridge.

There was another knock at the door.
"Now, who is it?" said Papa Wang. It was the Queen and her husband, the Duke. Papa Wang gasped.

The Queen opened the fridge. At first it was quiet. Then, "Go away, you great big spoon!" said the fridge.
"Our ears!" cried the Queen.
"There must be a mute button somewhere," said Papa Wang.

It was the end of the day. Everyone had gone home. Papa Wang went to get some butter for his toast. "Prune washer," said the fridge.

Papa Wang buttered his toast. Then he went to get some milk for his tea.
"Puke-for-brains," said the fridge.
"I'm tired of this!" said Papa Wang, while Yan tried hard not to giggle.

"I know just what to use," said Papa Wang. He grabbed the strongest glue he had. Then he glued the fridge door shut.

"There," said Papa Wang. "That will be the last we will hear from the fridge." Yan stopped playing the tune on her flute. She didn't really believe that the glue would work.

Papa Wang woke up late at night. He could hear a loud bumping sound coming from the fridge. The rude words were trying to get out!

"The fridge is going to blow up!" yelled Papa Wang. He picked the fridge up.
"I'm taking it away on my own. Do not argue," Papa Wang said to Yan.

Papa Wang tied the fridge to the top of his blue car. He used strong rope to make sure it was safe. Then he drove down the street.

Papa Wang was driving to the beach. The sand dunes looked red in the morning sunlight. "Are we there yet?" asked Yan.
"How long have you been back there?" yelled Papa Wang.

"This is dangerous, Yan," fumed Papa Wang. "This fridge is going to blow up!" There was a very loud bump from the fridge. Papa Wang stopped the car.

They got out of the car and looked up. The fridge was rocking and shaking. Papa Wang and Yan were too scared to move. They stood as still as statues.

Suddenly the Queen flew down from the sky. She had come to rescue them! What a relief! The Queen smiled at Papa Wang and Yan. Without saying a word, she picked the fridge up and flew upwards.

She continued to fly higher and higher. Soon, the Queen and the fridge were just a dot in the sky.

A huge BANG echoed across the sky as the fridge blew up. The word BUMS could be heard for miles around. Then milk, butter and carrots rained down from above.

Suddenly the Queen landed on Papa Wang.
She did not look amused.
"Thank you so much," said Yan.
"You are welcome," said the Queen, picking cheese out of her hair.

"We should go and get another fridge," said Papa Wang. But the car would not start. Papa Wang looked confused.

He opened his blue car to check what was wrong. "Toilet breath!" said the car.
"Come on, Yan, we are walking home," said Papa Wang. "I need a cup of tea and some peace and quiet!"

The Fridge is Being Rude

1. What was Papa Wang planning to do before Yan burst into the room?

2. How do you think everyone found out about the rude fridge?

3. How did Papa Wang try to stop the fridge from saying rude words?

    (a) Shout at it

    (b) Fill it up with food

    (c) Glue the door shut

4. Who flew down from the sky to help Papa Wang and Yan?

5. How do you think Papa Wang felt when the car started being rude? What would you have done with the rude car?

©2020 **BookLife Publishing Ltd.**
King's Lynn, Norfolk PE30 4LS

ISBN 978-1-83927-317-9

All rights reserved. Printed in Malaysia.
A catalogue record for this book is available from the British Library.

The Fridge is Being Rude
Written by John Wood
Illustrated by Chloe Jago

An Introduction to BookLife Readers...

Our Readers have been specifically created in line with the London Institute of Education's approach to book banding and are phonetically decodable and ordered to support each phase of the Letters and Sounds document.

Each book has been created to provide the best possible reading and learning experience. Our aim is to share our love of books with children, providing both emerging readers and prolific page-turners with beautiful books that are guaranteed to provoke interest and learning, regardless of ability.

BOOK BAND GRADED using the Institute of Education's approach to levelling.

PHONETICALLY DECODABLE supporting each phase of Letters and Sounds.

EXERCISES AND QUESTIONS to offer reinforcement and to ascertain comprehension.

BEAUTIFULLY ILLUSTRATED to inspire and provoke engagement, providing a variety of styles for the reader to enjoy whilst reading through the series.

**AUTHOR INSIGHT:
JOHN WOOD**

An incredibly creative and talented author, John Wood has written about 60 books for BookLife Publishing. Born in Warwickshire, he graduated with a BA in English Literature and English Language from De Montford University. During his studies, he learned about literature, styles of language, linguistic relativism, and psycholinguistics, which is the study of the effects of language on the brain. Thanks to his learnings, John successfully uses words that captivate and resonate with children and that will be sure to make them retain information. His stories are entertaining, memorable, and extremely fun to read.

This book is a 'b' level and is a purple level 8 book band.